SHORT BLACKS are gems of recent
Australian writing – brisk reads that quicken
the pulse and stimulate the mind.

SHORT BLACKS

BOOZE
TERRITORY

ANNA
KRIEN

SHORT  BLACKS

Published by Black Inc.,
an imprint of Schwartz Publishing Pty Ltd
37–39 Langridge Street
Collingwood VIC 3066 Australia
enquiries@blackincbooks.com
www.blackincbooks.com

First published in the *Monthly*, September 2011.
This edition published 2015.

National Library of Australia Cataloguing-in-Publication entry :
Krien, Anna, author. Booze territory / Anna Krien.
9781863957687 (paperback) 9781925203523 (ebook)
Short blacks ; no.6. Binge drinking–Northern Territory.
Drinking of alcoholic beverages–Northern Territory.
Indigenous peoples–Alcohol use–Northern Territory.
362.292089915

Cover and text design by Peter Long.

Printed in Australia by Griffin Press. The paper
this book is printed on is certified against the
Forest Stewardship Council® Standards. Griffin
Press holds FSC chain of custody certification
SGS-COC-005088. FSC promotes environmentally
responsible, socially beneficial and economically
viable management of the world's forests.

FSC
www.fsc.org
MIX
Paper from
responsible sources
FSC® C009448

ANNA KRIEN is the author of the award-winning *Night Games: Sex, Power and Sport*, *Into the Woods: The Battle for Tasmania's Forests* and the Quarterly Essay *Us and Them*.

On a Tuesday morning, I make my way to the Gap View Hotel for a drinking session starting at 10 am. I'm told this is one of Alice Springs' three notorious 'animal bars' but, when I get there, the hotel is all shut up. The car park is empty except for a car with an Aboriginal couple sitting inside. I tap on their window and wave my hand at the closed pub. "Not open?"

"2 pm," comes the answer.

"Oh," I nod. I'm about to get back into my car when I realise the woman is talking about the bottle shop.

"You mean the bottle shop isn't open till two?" I ask. She nods. "You waiting around for that?" She nods again. "Isn't there a bar here?" That's when I discover a section of the pub is open. The woman directs me out of the car park, back along the main road and down the side of the hotel. A small concrete corridor with no roof doglegs until it is hidden from street view, where a toothless security guard greets me. He raises an eyebrow, then runs a metal detector across my clothes and confiscates my pens.

"Someone's been stabbed with a pen before," he says. "You can grab 'em when you leave, luv."

Behind me an Aboriginal boy, just turned 18, offers a scrap of paper to prove he's of age. Kindly, the security guard explains how to get a proper ID and turns him away. I walk up a cement ramp to a bar, billiard tables and pokies. There are lots of people milling around but the guy at the entrance tells me it doesn't "get pumping till 11.30 am", when the bar "switches to full-strength beer". Techno music blares out of speakers. As I wander around, a Sudanese security guard approaches me, his face concerned. *Am I lost?* he wants to know.

In a way, I am. I don't want a beer. It's 10 am, for Chrissake.

*

At the Todd Tavern down the road it's just after midday and the place is jumping. Billy Joel is on the jukebox and women jiggle in time, waiting to be served. On one side of the tavern is the Riverside Bar, the original 'animal bar', complete with blackened windows creating a kind of false night for its drinkers, who chuck their empties into wheelie bins dotted around the room. A lone white man runs the bar.

"They're comfortable in there," numerous people say to me when I ask about the low-slung ceiling that makes you hunch and the permanent night. "No one *forces* them to drink there."

In 2009 CCTV footage revealed 236 people inside the small bar at 11.48 am when it is licensed for 100 – the Todd was suspended from trading for 5 days. Today, around the other side of the tavern, the cleaner and more sophisticated bar with clear windows is also full of Indigenous people. What used to be a voluntarily segregated pub – blacks in the animal bar, whites in the classier section – is now black and black.

Outside, Indigenous people are hanging around the closed roller doors of the Thirsty Camel drive-through bottle shop attached to the Todd Tavern. Some form small groups, others wait in banged-up cars across the road, and a lone man, his purple shirt tucked into black pants, his belt buckle and boots shining, with a cowboy hat tilted over his eyes, leans against the brick wall, waiting.

At 2 pm the shutters will open, the tavern will close and the drinking will shift to the dry riverbed of the Todd River.

The change in the hour brings about a different kind of busyness as pubs are cleaned for the late afternoon trade. It is rush hour for Alice Springs taxi drivers. "No car, no drive-through" is the new rule for these bottlos (unless you're white, in which case you can walk up and buy whatever you want), and taxis are hailed for the 10 metre trip and paid much, much more than the distance demands.

'Bush' minibuses that drive back and forth from remote Indigenous communities are cheered and hailed into the Gap View Hotel car park, the accordion doors opening for six or so blackfellas, some so zonked they can barely muster any sign of life. And then off they go! Through the drive-through!

I watch as the guy in the purple shirt and cowboy hat approaches the bottle shop and is shooed away like a feral dog. "No car, no drive-through," an attendant yells at the man's back as he slinks away.

*

Everywhere you drive along the Stuart Highway – the seam of bitumen connecting Darwin to Port Augusta – there are handshake agreements between roadhouses and local Indigenous communities. At the Marla Hotel, the last roadhouse in South Australia before the Territory, a young woman says it's "three cans per Aborigine, no glass, no spirits, and we write down all our takeaways". At the Mt Ebenezer Roadhouse, on the way to Uluru, it's no takeaways until the last tour bus has departed.

At Glendambo the bartender says he has to record all takeaway purchases greater than $100 in a book "that nobody reads", and has been told to ask all buyers, "especially Aborigines, if they're going onto APY lands" (the Anangu Pitjantjatjara Yankunytjatjara lands stretch over 100,000 square kilometres in north-west South Australia). But, he adds, "I don't, cos that's prejudiced." As part of the federal intervention, shops were asked to take down names of people who bought more than $100 worth of alcohol. Many retailers undermined this with $99 promotions, and the bookkeeping of one roadhouse reveals just how seriously the new rules have been taken there – apparently Sid Vicious, Rod Stewart and Charlie Brown have all come through. When I hear this, I cringe. Years ago, I signed in as Meryl Streep at Tennant Creek RSL.

In the long stretches between roadhouses I pass upside-down dead cows, hit by road trains and bloated like blimps; numerous abandoned cars, doors and boot wide open as if the occupants left in a rush; and the odd flock of fluorescent green budgies veering dangerously close to my windscreen. At night, the desert comes alive as Australia's mice plague starts to stir, the tiny rodents spilling like marbles across the road. In Aileron, a 17 metre statue of an Aborigine holding a spear stands on a hill overlooking the roadhouse. Inside, the manager is straight up: "A sixpack a day, takeaway, whether you're black or white."

Another 60 kilometres up the road I stop at Ti Tree Roadhouse. The owner refuses to speak to me but I learn from a man sitting outside that, for local Indigenous people, drinking is restricted to between 1.30 and 3.30 pm. "Sometimes the police do a roadblock between here and Alice Springs," he says, "only stopping cars with us [Aborigines] in them and they tip out all the alcohol on the spot. It doesn't matter where we're going, they tip it out." On a noticeboard outside the roadhouse, a faded newspaper clipping flutters. It's a Territory government notice. "We all love Alice Springs," it reads. "And we all want it to be a great place where we can live, work and raise a family. But there is no denying we've got some social problems right now."

As I near Alice Springs, I spend the night in a rest stop where several grey nomads are setting up. A woman from Cooktown in Far North

Queensland tells me about the first time she saw the robotic baby dummies that health workers are using to raise awareness among Aboriginal women about foetal alcohol syndrome. "There are two dummies," she says. "One's a healthy baby and the other has foetal alcohol syndrome. I saw them laid out next to each other on a trestle table. The alcohol baby's chest was all caved in and had these strange skinny limbs. Plus it has that weird cry alcohol babies have." She starts to make a sound like the agitated bleating of a lamb. "It won't stop."

In the early hours of the morning, the howling of dingoes wakes me. Young pups join in, their little voices breaking mid yowl.

*

"Oh, they've got some bloody good drinkers in the Northern Territory," sang Ted Egan, a folk musician whom the governor-general appointed in 2003 to be the Territory's administrator. His lyrics – as many Australians have known for a long time, and studies are beginning to affirm – are spot on. For nearly 30 years, the money spent per capita on alcohol in the Territory has been between 50% and 100% higher than in the rest of Australia. Similarly, while the national annual cost of alcohol-related harm is about $15 billion (which works out to be a little less than $1000 per adult), the figure for the Territory is more than $4000 per adult. The National Alcohol Beverage Industries Council counters these statistics. This body of alcohol manufacturers and sellers claims its own commissioned study shows more costs are borne by the individual, with national public costs at $3.8 billion. But whatever the overall cost, the Territory government figures are brutal. Alcohol-related crime and illness costs the region's public purse $642 million per year.

And, while deaths attributable to booze among non-Indigenous Australians in the Territory are *twice* the national rate, it's the drinking habits of the Indigenous population that really stand out.

In 2009, when asked about grog restrictions, Ernie Dingo, presenter of *The Great Outdoors*, bitterly told Western Australia's *Sunday Times* that Indigenous people are unfairly targeted because they're visible. "Aboriginal people are open people – if there's a drink and you don't want it in your house, you drink it in a public place," he said. "To us there is nothing wrong with that. But to other people, who are so far up themselves, who look at those drunken Aborigines out there, yet they go home and they are cupboard drinkers."

To a degree this is true. Just over 30% of people in the Northern Territory are Indigenous. In towns such as Tennant Creek, Indigenous people represent almost half of the population, whereas their representation in other states is less than 4%. It's also worth noting that, despite the stereotype that 'all Aborigines are drunks', the 2004–05 National Aboriginal and Torres Strait Islander Health Survey estimated that

16% of the Indigenous population engaged in risky drinking habits, which is a similar figure to the national average. However, a 2008 survey also revealed that nearly 40% of Indigenous Australians binge-drink, double the figure for non-Indigenous Australians.

A couple of years ago, a video posted on YouTube revealed two Territory cops pulling a drunk Aboriginal man to his feet, urging him to sing and dance while they filmed him on a mobile phone. 'Chappy' happily complied, breaking into 'Rivers of Babylon' then slurring "Happy Birthday, Blake" at their request. The cop filming turned the camera around to his face and proclaimed, "This shit is fucked up!" Rightly, the police were reprimanded – but there the matter stopped.

Then, of course, the ethics squad moved in. The editor of *The National Indigenous Times*, Chris Graham, felt that more needed to be done to punish the police. Writing in *Crikey*, he said that "only a very 'special' class of Australian would think it was appropriate to film it" and that the video was indicative of a wider racist "police culture". Much of what Graham wrote was valid *and* predictable – fuelling another unhelpful stereotype, that of the 'victim'. The reality is that Indigenous people who drink dangerously cause huge flow-on effects for the rest of the community. No claims of high visibility can explain away certain facts.

In the Territory, the rate of alcohol-related death among Indigenous people is nine to ten times higher than the national average. In town camps it is a daily struggle to stop dwellings of 15 or more people turning into a permanent house party. A local pastor in Alice Springs tells me that, in one such house, a teenage couple whose first child had been removed by welfare rolled on top of their second newborn during a drunken binge and suffocated the baby.

Among the biggest direct killers is alcoholic

liver cirrhosis. Between 2001 and 2005, the Australian Bureau of Statistics gathered data from Northern Territory, Queensland, South Australia and Western Australia, which showed liver disease accounted for 75% of deaths among Indigenous men aged between 35 and 54 years old. To compare, 8.8% of non-Indigenous male deaths in the age group were due to liver failure. For Indigenous females, the figure was 50.8%. Non-Indigenous females? 3.6%.

Yet there are other killers, too: one doctor mused that "for some reason, in Yuendumu, their hearts give up before their livers." Alcohol abuse also figures in car crashes, murders, bashings, sexual assaults, neglect and suicide. Toxicology reports show extremely high levels of alcohol in the bodies of most Indigenous people who have committed suicide – a dose of Dutch courage has teenagers kicking out chairs from underneath them, cords tied around their necks or, as in a few Top End communities, climbing up powerlines and electrocuting themselves by holding on to the cables.

"Don't Lose Yourself. *Don't Get Horrors*" is the slogan for an alcohol-awareness campaign across the Territory, and these are its horror stories. In the front yard of a house in Little Sisters town camp, Alice Springs, numerous electrical cords hang from the branches of a tree. The ends are frayed, wires showing, as residents keep cutting down women trying to hang themselves. In a camp of ten or so houses, the reminders of death loom large. Across the way, a white cross in another front yard marks where a woman crashed a car into a tree and died.

*

In 2007, after crown prosecutor Nanette Rogers spoke on national television about child sexual abuse in Indigenous communities and camps around Alice Springs, the *Little Children are Sacred* report stated – as had many previous reports – that tackling alcohol abuse had to become a top priority. Within months large blue and white signs were erected declaring a ban on alcohol and pornography in 'prescribed' areas. It was the very first initiative of the federal government's intervention – and, for the most part, a fairly easy call to make, considering most of the region's remote communities had been nominally dry for decades, though without sufficient policing to enforce this.

It was inevitable that residents of these communities had mixed feelings about the signs. Some said they felt "shamed" by them, that the government was making out that all Indigenous people are drunks and paedophiles. This was perhaps best expressed by the sign into Mutitjulu, on which someone graffitied "RACIST". Others saw the signs as a glimmer of hope – just maybe, they thought, help was finally on its way. But, strangely, for all its 'tough love' merits, the intervention seemed to sprint across Aboriginal land only to skid and brake at its boundaries. Beyond this line, where liquor outlets bloom, a much less popular fight was waiting to be had.

*

Winter in Alice Springs is beautiful. A crisp blue sky slowly thaws out the night as jade green parrots canoodle in white gum trees. At first glance, the place appears in much better shape than when I visited in 2005 and again in 2006. Back then the town of 21,622 people, a service hub to 240 remote communities, was becoming known as the stabbing capital of the world. Over seven years (1998–2005) doctors saw more than 200 knife victims per year, mostly Aboriginal and mostly women. Whilst Indigenous people represented 17% of the town's population, they accounted for 85% of *all* hospital admissions, the majority being alcohol-related.

At the time, locals reassured me the violence was "black on black", not anything for me to worry about – an Aboriginal woman was 24 times more likely to be attacked than I was. The main streets of Alice were dotted with gambling circles – people playing cards on the shuffle, others lurching from tourist to relative, humbugging for cash and accusing people of racism if they didn't part with a ciggie.

Today on the surface Alice seems calmer, but many claim the entrenched drinking problems have not been solved, rather 'moved along'. This, however, does not give credit to the town's attempts to deal with such a fraught and explosive issue. No less than 15 different restrictions have been rolled out across the town since 2002, with an alcohol management plan implemented by the Territory government in 2006. Mostly through the lobbying of a local alcohol policy group, the People's Alcohol Action Coalition (PAAC), Alice introduced a Banned Drinkers Register, curbed its bottle shop opening hours, banned 4 and 5 litre wine casks, and limited the takeaway sale of 2 litre casks and bottles of fortified wine to one per person per day after 6 pm.

For the first two years of the restrictions introduced in 2006, alcohol consumption dropped by almost 20% and murders and manslaughters halved compared with 2004–06. Some 70% of drinkers switched to beer and 85% moved away from cheap wine. Then, in 2009, consumption and serious assaults began to creep up again as retailers – particularly Coles – filled the void left behind by casks with bargain-priced cleanskins, many cheaper than a bottle of water. In spite of themselves, retailers couldn't help responding to the market. Today, as more Indigenous people take to walking about with 1.2 litre Coca-Cola bottles half-filled with rum, the Coles Express servo runs promotions for "four bottles of Coca-Cola for $9".

Wholesale figures collected by the Territory's Department of Justice reveal that consumption remains 14% below the pre-restrictions level, with the department also recording a steady decline in murders, suicides and stabbings. Nevertheless, you could be forgiven for thinking that little substantial has changed. There is still restlessness. Eyes on the roller doors of bottle shops. Safe in the arms of daylight, locals scurry around doing their chores. But as night descends, along with the mercury, campfires light up along the riverbed and civil surveillance well and truly dissipates.

An intense spike of crime over summer saw an extra 18 police flown in, mostly to deal with marauding groups of kids who were daring each other to steal cars, break into houses and schools, ramraid bottle shops, mug pedestrians and climb in through the roofs of pubs to drink spirits and put the empty bottles back on the shelf. Remote communities displaced by floods put extra pressure on the town. In the four weeks after Christmas, one licensee experienced 25 break-ins across his two clubs, while three tourists were bashed and one German woman was stabbed.

On 6 July, towards the end of my stay, a man walking home with a takeaway pizza was punched and kicked by Aboriginal teenagers, and his wallet was nicked; minutes later they returned for his pizza. Last year, an Aboriginal family found themselves trapped in their home after the front door was tied shut with a rope and their car was stolen and torched. The home owner said she was afraid the house would be set alight with them inside.

That old 'black on black' reassurance now longer seems to hold true; in response, there are rumblings among white locals. One Face-book group, "Alice Springs residents who have had ENOUGH!!", dismisses accusations of racism, claiming it's the threatening demeanour of a "certain segment of the population" that's racist. It took police intervention to stop another group, Action for Alice, from setting up vigilante groups to patrol the streets. In 2010 five young men known as the 'Ute Five' – all white and all drunk except for the 'designated' driver, who remained sober the entire night – were convicted of manslaughter after an evening of hooning around the sandbanks of the Todd River, scaring Aboriginal camps and driving over blankets, culminated in the fatal bashing of a 33-year-old Aboriginal man.

On the outskirts of town, well-trodden paths between bottle shops and drinking camps are still littered with port, sherry and wine bottles, beer cans, silver goon bags, and bourbon and Coca-Cola bottles licked clean by ants.

*

"I was racist when I didn't serve 'em, racist when I did, and now I'm racist because of the rules," the publican Peter Severin says with exasperation. For 53 years Severin has run beef cattle and a roadhouse at Curtin Springs Station, 80 kilometres from Uluru. A lush oasis in the desert, the station, with its aviary, green lawn and two wandering emus, is a welcome relief from the endless ticker tape of scrub and red dirt.

In their first year at Curtin, Severin and his wife saw six people on the road to Uluru. Today the bitumen sees hundreds of cars and coaches daily. Severin helped build up the local tourist industry, even putting in the now controversial climbers' chain up the rock. On the nearby Mt Conner are the scattered ashes of three generations of the Severin family. You could say that Severin belongs here. And yet the station is also in the heartland of several desert communities. On the inside seam of the Territory's southern border, Curtin Springs is flanked by South and Western Australia, home of the Western Desert language groups (APY lands).

At 83, Severin is one of the longest-serving publicans in the Territory and, like many outback publicans of his era, he has been accused of discriminating against and exploiting the local Indigenous community. "It's you people," he says, pointing a finger at me. His dog, an old stocky cattle dog, paws my jeans for attention, while Severin ticks me off. "You people in the city who don't know what you're talking about." We lean on his bar, behind which resides an assortment of bottled spirits, faded photos and jars of desert snakes and scorpions. After I scratch the old dog's head, it retreats to the cool corner beside the fridge, satisfied.

During the lead-up to the 1967 referendum that saw the majority of Australians vote for the inclusion of Aborigines in the census, racially based drinking restrictions across the country were lifted. "In the Territory, we like to call it the drinking-rights referendum," says Severin. "And it was you people in the city who did this to them. We couldn't vote in that referendum because we're not a state and we had all the blackfellas!" I protest a little at being lumped in with his idea of wrongdoing do-gooders but it's half-hearted. Even if I had been alive at the time, I doubt I'd have foreseen the ramifications of entangling drinking rights with equal rights.

"When the pubs open, so will the graves," Pastor Friedrich Wilhelm Albrecht at Finke River Mission had warned when protests around the country in the late '50s urged for equal rights, including the right to drink. At rallies many activists held up posters of the artist Albert Namatjira with the slogan "Citizenship ... control the liquor not the Aborigines". The painter had been arrested in 1958 for giving alcohol to a ward (most Indigenous people were considered 'wards' under the Welfare Ordinance) only a year after he had been anointed with 'white' citizenship. It was the second time he had had to face the law as a white man, after a court heard earlier that same year that the painter's new ability to procure alcohol led to a heavy drinking session in an Alice Springs town camp that resulted in the murder of a young and pregnant Aboriginal woman. A taxi driver had testified that he dropped Namatjira off at the camp on the night of the murder with a carton of beer, a bottle of Treasure Island rum and a flagon of wine.

A fighting fund was raised to fly a Melbourne QC to the Territory to appeal Namatjira's six-month sentence. But Martin Kriewaldt, the sole Supreme Court judge in the Territory at the time, did not drop the charges and instead reduced the sentence to three months. Committed to sobriety, Kriewaldt believed prohibition was a necessary measure to protect the Indigenous population on the way to assimilation. In his judicial remarks, he noted the disparity between the advocacy of those in the Territory and the urgings of urban activists. "Those of us who have lived for more than a year or two in the Territory," he wrote, "realise that legislation for the protection and advancement of Aborigines is essential if they are to escape extinction."

His ruling created a national uproar – and the drinking restrictions fell like dominos, state by state. In the Territory, the right to drink was granted to Indigenous people in 1964. Then, less than a year later, the equal-wage ruling saw Aboriginal stockmen lose their jobs. Many pastoralists baulked at hiring a black man for the price of a white man, while other pastoralists claimed their best Indigenous workers simply became useless once the grog flowed freely.

Peter Severin says he pretended not to notice the lifting of alcohol restrictions at Curtin Springs, refusing alcohol to local Indigenous people. In the early '80s he made an informal agreement with nearby Indigenous communities to continue this practice. But then, in 1988, the handshake deal soured.

"These two do-gooders came up from the city and tried to buy a local Aboriginal man a beer and I wouldn't serve him. The women went to Canberra and complained about discrimination. I was informed by the Minister for Aboriginal Affairs that if I didn't serve Aborigines alcohol,

I'd be taken to court for discrimination." Severin is quiet before laughing bitterly.

Straightening up, I look at Severin in surprise. I hadn't considered that. How to make an informal deal to ban drinkers and get around the *Racial Discrimination Act 1975*?

When Severin opened his bar to the Indigenous community, business boomed. "There'd be 90 to 120 blackfellas in here," he says, both of us looking around, as I try to work out how they would fit. "All of them were well behaved. It was only when they got out onto the road they'd start to fight." At the wettest point, Indigenous people accounted for most of the station's liquor trade and, while Severin pocketed the profits, local communities bore the brunt of the ensuing violence and road accidents. Amid several court actions and community objections to the liquor commission – all of them dismissed – Severin at one point offered to limit sales to one 4 litre cask of wine and one carton of beer *per person per day*.

Then, in 1990, more than 50 Aboriginal women gathered at a hairpin turn in the Lasseter Highway and marched to Curtin Springs Station to present a letter to Severin. In it, they pleaded with him to stop serving alcohol to Indigenous people. Standing outside the roadhouse, the women circled the petrol bowsers, singing and making speeches as open-mouthed tourists watched. It was the beginning of a fully fledged women-led campaign against Severin. When 13 deaths over a six-year period were directly linked to the sale of alcohol at Curtin, the women turned to the Human Rights and Equal Opportunity Commission, applying for a Special Measures Certificate to exempt Severin from any claims of racial discrimination should he stop selling to the Indigenous community. Under the direction of the commission, Severin agreed to two six-month trials: first, on-premises drinking between 1 pm and 4 pm only with no takeaway sales; then, no on-premises drinking but with takeaway sales of up to six cans per person per day available between 1 pm and 4 pm.

"It was hard at the start," recalls Severin. "But then more and more tourists started to stop by." And he says he started to enjoy the peace: "We didn't have to listen out for fights on the road anymore." In the first 12 months, alcohol-related admissions to the health clinics in nearby Indigenous communities halved. After the trials Severin surprised the women by offering an option of no sales of alcohol to members of their community. In the years since, the Indigenous communities and Curtin Springs Station have lived side by side in relative peace – by returning to total prohibition.

*

From first contact the attempt to control the flow of alcohol into Indigenous communities has been fraught. In *First Taste: How Indigenous Australians Learned About Grog*, anthropologist

Maggie Brady describes colonists giving alcohol to Indigenous people sporadically, sometimes in an attempt to make a connection, at other times for the amusement of a crowd, encouraging them to fight each other. As the frontier grew, the insidious need for grog led to slave labour and the prostitution of Aboriginal women. Brady wonders if "perhaps, over time, Aboriginal drinking would have settled down ... But once alcohol was forbidden, it took on a new power."

Of course, there were always whites willing to supply alcohol in spite of prohibition but the transactions continued to be brusque and predatory, while the civil norms of the local pub were forbidden to Aboriginal drinkers. "Banning Aboriginal and Torres Strait Islander people from hotels," Brady writes, "turned drinking *inwards*, instead of opening it up." When the restrictions were lifted, remote communities were encouraged to set up 'wet' canteens and clubs to learn 'how to drink' – most of these were in Queensland and Western Australia. In some communities, sirens signalled the start of the daily drinking sessions, and traditional ceremonies were cut short. Often located 200 or more kilometres from the nearest towns, these wet canteens were rarely, if ever, monitored to see if they complied with liquor laws. An even more perverse reality set in when it became clear these waterholes often represented the *only* real economy: the addiction grew, not only to the booze but also to the profits.

The ABC's *Four Corners* visited Aurukun in Far North Queensland three times over four decades to document the effects of grog. In 1978 the reporter Maryanne Smith revealed a community desperately trying to keep alcohol addiction at bay while a minister under the Bjelke-Petersen government – which was adamantly opposed to land rights and keen to open up the area for mining – pushed for a wet canteen.

MARYANNE SMITH: Why is it then that you've suggested that they can have a canteen?

MINISTER RUSS HINZE: Yeah, but now, did I suggest that?

SMITH: Well, indeed they said you did. They said that you told them now they have local government they're entitled to have a wet canteen ...

HINZE: If they want it. You see the Australian — the Queensland government are not going to be seen in the eyes of the world as taking a part of Queensland and saying you can't take liquor there.

SMITH: But the people at Aurukun say they don't want a wet canteen ...

HINZE: OK.

SMITH: It was you who suggested it.

HINZE: No, I didn't. I said if they want it.

Reverend John Adams remembered the meeting between Aurukun elders and Minister

Hinze quite differently. According to Adams, Hinze told Aurukun there should be a wet canteen because white contractors had a right to drink. Then, after the community had held out for seven years, several drinkers were voted onto council in 1985 and almost immediately, without consultation, Carlton & United Breweries opened a canteen in the middle of the local park among the children's play equipment. Within five years *Four Corners* returned, by which time the murder rate in Aurukun had reached 120 times the Queensland average. Three years ago the Queensland government shut down the council-run Three Rivers Tavern in the face of local opposition.

Today many people blame overcrowding and crime in Alice Springs and Katherine, as well as Darwin, on the intervention's alcohol bans – essentially, the belated enforcement of decades-old bans. Indigenous people have apparently swarmed to these centres in search of alcohol. Early this year, there were calls for remote communities to set up – yep – wet canteens. The mayor of Katherine, Anne Shepherd, backed the calls, saying drinking should be "controlled and designed by communities themselves". But 'urban drift', as it is called in the north, is not a new phenomenon. The intervention has simply exacerbated it. "We call it moth syndrome," says one health worker, because young Indigenous people, like almost all young people in rural areas, are attracted to the lights.

Ultimately this renewed call for wet canteens is akin to sending people back from an idea of a future. Even if people have arrived in town primarily for the booze, a rare chance may present itself to redirect that ambition.

On 1 July the government rolled out new alcohol restrictions – the toughest in Australia – across the Territory. Anyone wanting to buy takeaway

alcohol has to have an identification card, which is scanned to ensure banned drinkers are not purchasing grog. The Banned Drinkers Register includes people taken into protective custody to sober up at least three times in three months, those who have committed alcohol-fuelled crime and drink drivers who blow over 0.15.

Banned drinkers can reduce the length of their suspension by attending rehabilitation. In Darwin and Alice Springs, an Alcohol and Other Drugs Tribunal has been set up to review the register, while a specialist court is geared towards rehabilitation and case management for substance-dependent offenders. In addition to the register, alcoholics who are violent or neglect their kids could have their welfare payments quarantined. Curiously, Territorians can also ask to be on the banned register.

Of all days to launch the Territory-wide scanner system 1 July was a bold choice. Marking self-government in 1978, it is 'Territory Day'.

However, while bottle shop owners learning to use the new system complained about queues and impatient customers, for the most part the system was launched without a hitch. More than 43,000 people were scanned between Friday and Sunday night, with five refused service. By the end of the weekend, 63 names had been added to the list, a young female driver becoming the lucky first after she blew a blood-alcohol reading of 0.237.

If you add to this register the complex system of dry areas and unique town rules across the region, as well as voluntary withdrawal by retailers of cask wine, the sale of fortified wine only after 6 pm, schemes to buy back liquor licences, the placement of scanners at the entrances of 'problem' bars, amended opening hours, individuals declaring their homes dry by placing signs on the front fence and informal handshake agreements between publicans *and* remote Indigenous communities that spill over the Territory border into South Australia, Western Australia and Queensland, you may well have the beginnings of the alcohol industry's worst nightmare.

*

"Today is Territory Day, a time to celebrate *self-determination* and our great Territory lifestyle," said the Country Liberals' shadow minister for alcohol policy, Peter Styles, on 1 July (italics mine). "But under Labor our rights, freedoms and lifestyle are being taken away, bit by bit." This is the great irony facing Indigenous people in the Territory and beyond: right-wing ideologues using terminology such as 'self-determination' and left-wing ideologues huffing about 'human rights', with regards to the intervention's temporary acquisition of land rights and micromanagement of welfare monies. Both sides have cataracts and neither sentiment is helpful at the 'pointy end' of the issue, where Reverend Basil Schild works. "The death end," as the Lutheran pastor explains.

At the Alice Springs cemetery, Schild – a youngish man with dark blond hair – flits from grave to grave, studying the inscriptions. Sometimes, when people ask what he does for a living, he simply says, "I bury black people."

"A funeral procession will start at the gates here," Schild tells me, "with me walking in front of the hearse while a large group of people gather behind it. It's usually a sunny day like this and I'm thinking, what the hell am I doing here *again*?"

One morning recently, as Schild was fiddling with his car radio, he got a fright when he heard the local shock jock mention his name as someone lobbying sellers of alcohol to take greater responsibility. "People were calling in, abusing me," he says, somewhat wide-eyed. "But I work at the death end of all this. I've met ten-year-old kids who have been to more funerals than any white kid would go to in their lifetime. While they're still waiting for Gran to die, an Aboriginal kid has been to up to 100 funerals."

Schild has no time for locals complaining about 'responsible' drinkers being inconvenienced for the sake of a minority of 'problem' drinkers, or the poor pensioner who cannot buy their tipple of port until 6 pm, or the shift workers who deserve to be able to order a drink at 10 am. "Let's talk about a real problem," he says, firing up. "I buried the fifth son of an Aboriginal woman a few weeks ago, and that was her last. And this —" He points to the graves around us, the rows of deceased babies, teenagers and 20- to 30-year-olds: "This is just Alice. Most are buried back in their remote community. In some places you can see fresh graves in all directions." Nor is Schild enamoured of the criticism of income management. "Now this is picking a fight with the human rights lobby but welfare shouldn't be spent on alcohol."

Trevor Porter, the manager of Heavitree Gap Tavern, agrees. One of the three so-called problem bars, Heavitree Gap is the least 'animal'-esque.

An ordinary-looking place, it recently acceded to pressure and pushed the opening hour to 11 am. There's not enough income management, as far as Porter is concerned. "They're still in here, day in and day out," he says. "The money seems endless."

Schild wants the morning booze trade in Alice to cease. "Licensees say that people don't get there till 10.30 now and only drink light beer until 11.30 when the heavy beer starts up. They're trying to imply there's not much money made in the morning. Well, if that's the case, then why not cut your losses and shut shop?" A sober morning would give the drinker *and* the money a chance to be intercepted. "At the moment, if you don't get them by 9.30 in the morning, you've missed them. I've arrived in town camps at that time and been asked by stragglers, 'What you doing here? You're too late, everyone gone.'"

However, a recent attempt by PAAC to curtail the morning trade caused an uproar in Alice, with a "Drinkers' Rights" petition garnering more than 4000 signatures. The level of vitriol levelled at the lobbyist was staggering. PAAC quickly changed tack. Dr John Boffa, the group's spokesperson, says they have only two more cards to play: firstly, linking an alcohol-free day to welfare payments; secondly, controlling the price.

*

"It's the missing link. It hasn't been used as a lever until now," says Dr Boffa. I'm in his medical rooms on the day Alice Springs' two biggest supermarkets, Coles and Woolworths, announce they will no longer sell bottles of wine for less than $8, and will withdraw 2 litre casks from sale. In between speaking to me, an excited Boffa juggles phone calls from ABC Radio. As I listen in, it appears the 'wine bladder' is on borrowed time.

"We just felt it was the right thing to do," says Ian McLeod, managing director of Coles, to

ABC Radio, adding that the company will cease offering national promotions and discounts in Alice Springs.

After that, liquor outlets across town fell into line, withdrawing excessively cheap wine from their shelves, with only the Todd and Gap View bottle shops holding out. Both licensees say they fear losing sales to the internet, while one frustrated publican told Boffa he was going too far and putting himself at risk from some very angry drinkers. But the doctor laughs this off.

Oddly, as pressure mounted on the two remaining pubs, the Alice Springs Town Council weighed in. In a letter to local supermarkets (that the mayor did not want to put his name to after voting against the motion), the council asked that their decision not to sell cheap and cask wine be reversed.

The most vocal advocate of the council motion, Murray Stewart, told the ABC that controlling the price would have no effect on the town's drinkers and would penalise the majority for a minority. "You cannot price them into behavioural change," he said. "That comes through strong rehabilitation and all you do is make a desperate person more desperate." He also raised concerns that Aboriginal women would be more at risk of glassing in the absence of casks.

Stewart's argument runs counter to mounting evidence from all around the world that higher pricing is, in fact, more effective than any other measure. "Comprehensive reviews of the evidence show that, by themselves, alcohol education programs are ineffective," says Dr Steven Skov of the Territory's health department. The World Health Organization cites over 50 studies conducted in multiple countries that reveal an increase in price significantly limits alcohol abuse. But the question remains, should the pricing be controlled by taxes (nanny state!) or subject to voluntary regulation?

You need only look back to what is now considered England's first public health campaign in the mid 1700s, when the 'gin craze' had London in a state of chaos and elevated crime, creating the first documented cases of foetal alcohol syndrome. In a time of upheaval, as more and more people were displaced from their rural homes, the ready availability of gin in the city (sellers were pushing around wheelbarrows of the stuff) filled a lonely void. To cope, the British government introduced a range of taxes, legislation and licenses, the strategy at times belated and clumsy, with people – now officially gin addicts – rioting in response to any meddling with supply. It took more than 20 years, a 1000% increase in gin taxes *plus* a failed series of wheat crops (which pushed the spirit's price up) to quench the city's thirst.

In Alice Springs PAAC is busy pushing for a minimum floor price. Many alcohol retailers – even the Territory branch of the Australian Hotels Association – are onside. "A floor price is the best way to address alcohol-related issues, it reduces problem drinking, it stops problem products entering the market, and because it only affects the bottom 2% of products, responsible drinkers will never notice the difference!" wrote one supermarket manager to the *Alice Springs News*. But there is another, more conniving argument for a floor price. Critics say the incremental price hike will simply put more money in the pockets of retailers. Delia Lawrie, the Territory's treasurer and alcohol policy minister, agrees.

As it stands, Australia's tax system awards beer producers for lowering alcohol content. In 2007, Foster's dropped the alcohol in VB from 4.9% to 4.8% and saved $20 million per year. Bizarrely, though, wine is not taxed on its alcohol content but on its wholesale price. So, while full-strength beer is taxed an approximate 39 cents per standard drink (a drink containing ten grams of alcohol), cask wine is taxed 6 cents and bottled wine 26 cents per standard drink – and there are rebates for smaller producers. Combine this with a 'wine lake' (caused by a decade-long glut of grapes) and you have retailers selling cleanskins for less than a bottle of water and 5 litre casks going for 8 bucks. Cirrhosis of the liver, anyone?

Last year the Henry Tax Review recommended an overhaul of Australia's alcohol taxation to replace the hodgepodge of 13 different rates with a 'volumetric tax', under which *alcohol will be alcohol*, no matter the type of drink it appears in. This July, as the Banned Drinkers Register was rolled out, the National Alliance for Action on Alcohol – a coalition of doctors, health policy experts and organisations, social workers and medico groups – converged in Canberra to lobby politicians for the volumetric tax. Minister Lawrie has said the Territory government is also lobbying for a volumetric tax as opposed to a floor price as it would put revenue into the pockets of governments rather than retailers –

revenue that could go towards counteracting the social costs of alcohol abuse.

John Pollaers, the CEO of Foster's Group, sees the volumetric tax as an important element of social policy but also wants regulators to be able to target specific dangerous drinking patterns, such as those involving spirits and their underage accomplice, alco-pops. He adds that the majority of alcohol producers are for a volumetric tax, "with cheap wine and cask wine holding out".

*

"We oppose both a minimum floor price and volumetric tax. We don't believe in trying to control social problems by taxation," asserts Anita Poddar, spokeswoman for Accolade Wines, Australia's largest wine company, with brands including cask producers Stanley, Hardys and Berri. I've already pissed Poddar off by going over her head to the CEO, arranging an interview that I suspect she neatly nipped in the bud – his secretary suddenly explained he had been called into an "urgent meeting" and put me through to Poddar.

"Looks like you've been bumped back to me after all," she said, her glee detectable.

"Yep, funny that," I replied, preparing myself for the usual stiff monologue, but then she made a point that took me by surprise.

"Taxation is not a means to control social issues," Poddar repeated forcefully. "We believe in education. Look at skin melanomas."

"What?"

"They're on the decrease in Australia. Education worked for skin cancer and we didn't tax people for going out in the sun."

Now, until someone proves to me that there is a conglomerate behind the sun earning millions of dollars from people soaking up its rays, I'm going to conclude from this that Australia's wine industry is very, *very* scared. When I ask if the alcohol industry feels it is next in line for the equivalent of the restrictions on tobacco, Poddar is tight-lipped. "I won't be going into my own opinion on that, but yes, it has been suggested."

Back at Foster's, Pollaers is more responsive. "There needs to be a paradigm shift within the alcohol industry to stop thinking of lobbyists as anti-alcohol, but as pro-family, pro-health and pro-human rights."

When I drove home from Alice Springs, through South Australia's opal towns, along the weave of wine valleys and cellar doors into Melbourne, I realised that alcohol and the problems in Indigenous communities is only part of the story. Alcohol is suddenly downwind from those banished smokers and the industry has been dreading a backlash against it for years. In January 2010, police in New South Wales emailed hundreds of pubs and bottle shops asking them not to sell most lines of full-strength beer, wine and spirits before 2 pm on Australia Day, with a further request to refrain from serving shots and drinks with an alcohol content greater than 5% after 9 pm. The police claimed the public holiday had gone from a celebration to a day of drunken violence. A few years prior, the City of Sydney introduced a 2 am lockout for certain nightclubs after local hospitals reported at least half of all admitted assaults were alcohol related. In Byron Bay, a favourite tourist destination with three times the state's average of alcohol-related violence, locals are protesting against plans for a supersized discount bottle shop.

Two nights after I arrived home, I stood on platform nine of Richmond Station, a central artery for the flow of the city's commuters, and looked up to see a backlit billboard swivelling above me. On one side it read, "ALCOHOL DOES NOT CAUSE VIOLENCE", then spun to reveal "BLAME AND PUNISH THE INDIVIDUAL". The spinning mantra – oddly reminiscent of America's famous gun-lobbyist line, "Guns don't kill people, people kill people" – provides no indication of whose message this is. In fact, it appears so omnisciently against the skyline that it could be a message from God himself.

*

In 1971 the American anthropologist Nancy Lurie wrote of the heavy and harmful drinking among native North Americans as "the world's oldest ongoing protest demonstration", describing it as a "protest in order to maintain the Indian–white boundary". It's not difficult to draw a similar conclusion here. The nihilism that accompanies these alcohol-fuelled stories is a rejection of us, of this society.

The river of grog flows *between* us.

Dr Boffa says the PAAC will rejoin efforts to prevent alcohol abuse in Indigenous communities once Alice Springs has an alcohol-free day and a price on booze. "Fixing the problem of alcohol abuse will not solve everything," he says, "but if it's not addressed, it will wreck every other effort." In particular PAAC intends to work on early childhood development. "It's in a child's first three years, that's when you can make a difference."

When I stand under the billboard at Richmond Station, red desert dust still beneath my nails, I remember my university days of reading psychoanalysis, especially the Freudian notion that a child is cast in bronze by the time they're five years old. I *loved* alcohol when I was a teenager. From about age 12, I drank as much as I could get my hands on. I stole it out of the fridge, thieved it from shops, snatched it out of hands, drank vanilla essence at people's houses and mixed up rocket fuel whenever I could. In fact, there is quite a lot I don't remember about my teens, including losing my virginity or what I took that night that saw me having to strip off shit-stained clothes in a side street. But I had one thing locked inside of me: *a homing device*.

I wonder if this is what being cast in bronze means. I always had a sense of sanctuary. Even in my blackouts I managed to find my way home. I wove across highways in high heels to a dimly remembered time of feeling safe.

As my train comes, I get a taste of bile, a flash of anger at the old guard, Left and Right, at their egos, their rhetoric and at an intervention that hasn't intervened anywhere near enough. "What frigging intervention?" Reverend Schild said to me as we drove past the bars brimming in the morning and the gathering, hollowed-out shadow people, watching the roller doors of the bottle shops.

Richard Flanagan's perceptive, hilarious, searing exposé of the conformity that afflicts our public life.

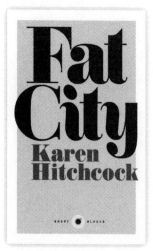

In a riveting blend of story and analysis, doctor and writer Karen Hitchcock explores chemistry, psychology and impulse to excess to explain the West's growing obesity epidemic.

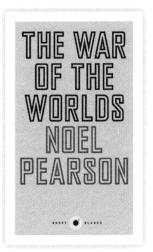

Noel Pearson considers
the most confronting issue
of Australian history:
the question of genocide,
in early Tasmania
and elsewhere.

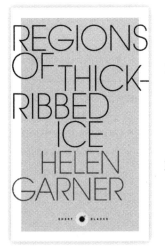

Helen Garner tells the tale
of a journey to Antarctica
aboard the *Professor
Molchanov*, spanning
icebergs, tourism, time,
photography and the many
forms of desolation.

John Birmingham's
unflinching account
of the Indonesian
Army's Battalion 745 as
it withdrew from East
Timor after the 1999
independence vote, leaving
a trail of devastation
in its wake.

Anna Krien takes a
clear-eyed look at
Indigenous binge-drinking,
and never fails to see
the human dimension of
an intractable problem,
shining a light on its
deep causes.

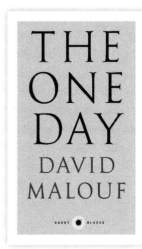

David Malouf traces the meaning of Anzac Day and shows how what was once history has now passed into legend, and how we have found in Anzac Day 'a truly national occasion.'

Simon Leys' exceptionally beautiful and elegiac essay about a summer spent on the crew of a tuna-fishing boat in Brittany.

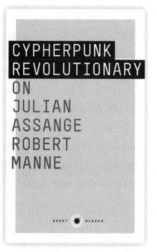

Robert Manne reveals the making of Julian Assange and shows how he became one of the most influential Australians of our time.

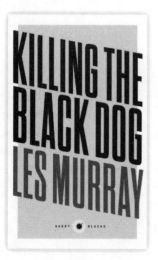

Les Murray's frank and courageous account of his struggle with depression.

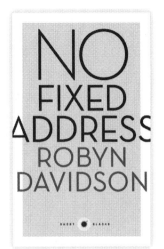

Robyn Davidson's fascinating and moving essay about nomads explores why, in times of environmental peril, the nomadic way with nature still offers valuable lessons.

Galarrwuy Yunupingu tells of his early life, his dealings with prime minsters, and how he learnt that nothing is ever what it seems.